はしがき

　本書は、Voice of America（VOA）の Learning English から特に健康と環境分野を扱っている素材を厳選して英語教材としたものです。

　これまで同テーマの教材を出版して参りましたが、2016 年度に第 10 作を刊行したのを機に、本文のレイアウトと表紙デザインを一新して見やすさにも配慮し、VOA Health & Environment Reports のシリーズタイトルでの刊行を　　　　　　　　　　　　　　　　　の Volume 4 になります。

　この教材で取り上げられてい　　　　　　　　　　　　　　規模のものまでと幅広く、学生の皆さんも飽きることなく興味を持　　　　　　　　　　　　　　　力養成に最適な教材です。

　VOA Learning English は非英　　　　　　　　　　　　　　entic material であり、取り上げられているトピックは最新のニュースです。Learning English のニュースはナチュラルスピードの 3 分の 2 の速度で読まれていますが、不自然なものではなく、リスニング力の養成に適しています。本書には、実際に放送された音声だけでなく、ネイティブ・スピーカーによってナチュラルスピードで吹き替えられた音声も用意されています。Learning English の基本使用語彙は 1,500 語程度ですが、それ以外の語には Notes に解説を付けています。

　本書は、pre-listening、while-listening、post-listening の各段階で、語彙、大意把握、内容把握、イディオムや一般的な表現の確認、英語表現のタスクを課しています。

□ Title・関連写真・概要：ユニットのタイトルや関連写真や概要によって、トピック内容に対する学生の皆さんのスキーマ（背景知識）を活性化し、トピック内容の理解に対する動機付けとなります。

□ Vocabulary: 本文中の語の語義としてふさわしい定義を選択します。英語を英語で理解することによってトピックの内容理解への手がかりが得られることになります。

□ Summary Check: 1st Listening の後、ここでトピック内容の大まかな概要を把握して下さい。

□ 2nd Listening: 本文中の空所に聴き取った語を入れることによって細かな内容理解を確認します。空所箇所は、トピック内容のキーワードを中心に、聴き取りにくい箇所にも設定しています。

□ True or False?: トピック内容の把握についてその正誤を確認します。

□ Useful Expressions: 本文に出現したイディオムや一般的な表現の確認を行います。

□ Translations: Vocabulary で取り上げた語句の並べ替えによる英作文を行います。トピック内容に関連するものとなっています。

□ 無料音声ダウンロード：リスニング活動は授業中だけでなく授業以外でも自主的に取り組むことが必要です。http://shohakusha.com/free/sound からダウンロードした音声を十分に活用して下さい。

　本書を用いた学習と並行して VOA のサイト（http://www.voanews.com）へアクセスして最新のニュースを視聴されることをお勧めします。

　最後になりますが、本書の出版をお勧め頂いた松柏社社長森信久氏に対して心から御礼を申し上げます。

安浪誠祐

Richard S. Lavin

Contents

Woof! I Feel Stress, Too!

犬の飼い主がストレスを感じると
犬もまたそれを感じることがわ
かった。体内で放出される化学物
質の濃度が関係しているという。

VOCABULARY

下の単語を本文中に探し、(a) 〜 (e) の中から語義としてふさわしいものをそれぞれ選びなさ
い。

1) unemployment　　**2)** personality　　**3)** director

4) continually　　**5)** resemble

(a) the state of not having a job
(b) to look like or be like
(c) the leader of a company or organization
(d) the way someone is or generally behaves
(e) again and again

◀)) 1st Listening　　まず VOA ニュースを聴きましょう。

SUMMARY CHECK

ニュースの概要として最もふさわしいものを下の 1) 〜 4) のなかから選びなさい。

1) Dogs seem friendly, but they are not interested in humans.
2) Border collies understand humans better than Shetland sheepdogs do.
3) A study suggests that a dog's emotional state is influenced by that of its owner.
4) Alicia Buttner recently found a job at the Nebraska Humane Society in Omaha.

📝 **Notes**

　When dog owners experience a long period of stress, they are not (¹　　　　) in feeling the pressure. Their dogs feel it, too.

　That information comes from a new study (²　　　　) Thursday in *Scientific Reports*.

Scientific Reports: 『サイエンティフィック・リポーツ』誌（オープンアクセスの電子ジャーナル）

　Swedish scientists centered the research on 58 people who (³　　　　) border collies or Shetland sheepdogs. Both are traditionally herding dogs.

herding dog: 牧畜犬

　The scientists (⁴　　　　) hair from the dog owners and their dogs. They looked at the levels of a hormone (⁵　　　　) cortisol. This chemical is released into the bloodstream during stressful experiences. Pieces of hair can take in this chemical.

level: 濃度
hormone: ホルモン
cortisol: コルチゾール
chemical: 化学物質

take in: ～を取り込む

　Depression, extreme (⁶　　　　) exercise and unemployment are just a few examples of stress causers that can affect the amount of cortisol released in humans, said Lina Roth of Sweden's Linkoping University.

　Roth and her team found that cortisol levels in the hair of dog owners closely (⁷　　　　) levels found in their dogs. The researchers say this suggests their stress levels were in sync — or (⁸　　　　).

　Roth believes that the owners are influencing the dogs (⁹　　　　) of dogs influencing their human owners. That is because there are human personality traits that also appear to (¹⁰　　　　) dogs' cortisol levels.

trait: 特性

　But why is it that people influence their dogs and not the other way around? It could be, Roth said in an email, because people are "a more (¹¹　　　　) part of the dog's life, whereas we humans also have other social networks."

　The study results are no (¹²　　　　), said Alicia Buttner. She is director of animal behavior with the

Nebraska Humane Society in the American city of Omaha.

Buttner said new evidence is continually found to show people and their dogs have extremely "close (¹³　　　)

35　that resemble the ones that parents share with their children."

Buttner also said there is not enough evidence to (¹⁴　　　) that the influence goes only one way.

She said, "It's not just as (¹⁵　　　) as owner gets

40　stressed, dog gets stressed."

Buttner said cortisol levels do not (¹⁶　　　) demonstrate "bad" stress. They instead can be (¹⁷　　　) of a good experience like getting ready to go for a walk, she said.

45　Roth and her team plan to (¹⁸　　　) whether other kinds of dogs react to their owners the same way.

For now, she offers advice for reducing how much stress a dog owner may be (¹⁹　　　) their pet. Dogs that play more show fewer signs of stress, she said.

50　So "just be with your dog and have (²⁰　　　)," Roth said.

Nebraska Humane Society: ネブラスカ・ヒューメイン・ソサイアティ（アメリカの動物保護団体）

sign: 兆候

★ TRUE OR FALSE?

1) ～ 5) のなかからニュースの内容として正しいものには T、間違っているものには F を選びなさい。

1) The research described involved more than one kind of dog.
2) The research involved checking cortisone levels.
3) Lina Roth thinks that the key problem is that dogs' stress is causing stress in their owners.
4) Alicia Buttner finds the results very surprising.
5) Cortisol is not always bad.

★ USEFUL EXPRESSIONS

日本語に合うように (　　　) を埋めなさい。

1) 健康を改善するための典型的な助言には身体的活動を増やすことがある。

   Typical (　　　　　　　　) for improving one's health includes increasing physical activity.

2) プロの翻訳家は通常外国語から母語に翻訳するが、通常その逆はない。

   Professional translators usually translate from a foreign language to their native language and usually not the other (　　　　　　) around.

3) すべての人の要求を満たすのに十分な真水は世界には存在しない。

   There is not (　　　　　　) fresh water in the world to meet everyone's needs.

4) ダックスフントやチワワやトイ・プードルは、日本で人気のある犬種のごくわずかな例である。

   The Dachshund, the Chihuahua, and the Toy Poodle are just a (　　　　　　) examples of dog breeds that are popular in Japan.

★ TRANSLATIONS

日本語に合うように (　　　) の語句を並び替えて、文を完成させなさい。

1) 犬と一緒にいるとき、犬がいろいろな意味で人間と似ていることを常に気づかされる。

   When spending time with dogs, we (are / are / continually / in many / reminded / similar / that they / to humans) ways.

   _____

   _____

2) ペットは幾つかの点で飼い主に似てくるとよく言われる。

   It (come / is / often / resemble / said / that pets / their owners / to) in some respects.

   _____

   _____

Unit 2 Good for You, Good for the Planet?

人間と地球にとって最良の食べ物が発見された。人間にとっては健康、地球にとっては環境に関わると考えられる。

VOCABULARY

下の単語を本文中に探し、(a) ～ (e) の中から語義としてふさわしいものをそれぞれ選びなさい。

1) diet 　　　　 2) prevent 　　　　 3) expert

4) professor 　　　 5) dairy

(a) the foods that a person or animal eats regularly
(b) a person with special knowledge or training
(c) milk and milk products
(d) a university teacher
(e) to stop something happening

🔊 1st Listening 　　 まず VOA ニュースを聴きましょう。

SUMMARY CHECK

ニュースの概要として最もふさわしいものを下の 1) ～ 4) のなかから選びなさい。

1) When choosing a diet, it is necessary to choose between personal and planetary health.
2) London is the leading research city for dietary studies.
3) It would be preferable for everyone to eat more cassave and potatoes.
4) A new diet may be good for the environment and for human health.

📝 **Notes**

Scientists in London say they have (¹　　　　) the best diet for both humans and the planet.

If the world (²　　　　) the so-called "planetary health" diet, the scientists told Reuters that each year more than
5 11 million early (³　　　　) could be prevented.

For the health of the planet, they (⁴　　　　) the same diet would reduce greenhouse gases and save more land, water and animals.

This new food plan is the (⁵　　　　) of a three-year
10 project organized by *The Lancet* health journal. It (⁶　　　　) 37 experts from 16 countries.

Tim Lang, a professor at Britain's University of London, co-led the research. He told Reuters, "The food we eat and how we produce it (⁷　　　　) the health of people and the
15 planet, and we are currently getting this (⁸　　　　) wrong."

Lang added that the world's population is (⁹　　　　) to grow to 10 billion people by 2050. If we want to (¹⁰　　　　) everyone, he explained, we all need to change what we eat
20 and the way we eat by "improving food production and reducing food (¹¹　　　　)."

So, what do you eat on the planetary health diet?

The scientists who (¹²　　　　) this diet say it is largely plant-based but still has small amounts of dairy, fish and
25 meat. The diet calls for cutting red meat and sugar by 50 percent and (¹³　　　　) the amount of nuts, fruits, vegetables and legumes.

Food situations around the world are not (¹⁴　　　　). In certain areas, this would mean great changes. People in
30 North America, for example, eat 6.5 times the (¹⁵　　　　) amount of red meat. On the other hand, people in South

greenhouse gas: 温室効果ガス

The Lancet: 『ランセット』誌（医学雑誌）

Reuters: ロイター通信社（イギリスの通信社）

legume: 豆

Asia eat only half the amount suggested by the new planetary health diet.

Meeting the (¹⁶   ) for vegetables would need big

35 changes in other areas. In sub-Saharan Africa, people on average eat 7.5 times the suggested amount of vegetables like potatoes and cassava.

sub-Saharan: サハラ砂漠以南の

cassava: キャッサバイモ（タピオカの原料）

Walter Willet of Harvard University in the United States also (¹⁷   ) to Reuters about the planetary

40 health diet. He said that more than 800 million people around the world do not get (¹⁸   ) food while many more have very unhealthy diets.

The scientists admit their goal will be difficult to (¹⁹   ). But for them doing nothing is also not an

45 (²⁰   ). Willet said, "If we can't quite make it, it's better to try and get as close as we can."

★ TRUE OR FALSE?

1) ～ 5) のなかからニュースの内容として正しいものには T、間違っているものには F を選びなさい。

1) Some scientists say that following the planetary health diet could prevent more than 11,000,000 early deaths.
2) *The Lancet* was involved in the planetary health diet project.
3) Reducing food waste is not part of the planetary health diet project.
4) A necessary measure in North America will be to reduce the amount of red meat that people eat.
5) According to Walter Willett, the number of people in the world who do not get enough food is about 80,000,000.

★ USEFUL EXPRESSIONS

日本語に合うように（　　　）を埋めなさい。

1) 油断していたら、列車に乗り遅れるよ。できるだけ速く走って。

   If you're not careful, you're going to miss the train. Run as fast
   (　　　　　　) you can!

2) 日本における塩分の毎日の平均消費量は WHO に推奨された量の２倍以上であることが分かった。

   It has been found that the average daily consumption of salt in Japan is
   more than two (　　　　　　) the amount recommended by the WHO.

3) アメリカのグリーン・ニュー・ディールは 2030 年までに化石燃料使用を止めることを提唱する。

   The Green New Deal in the U.S. (　　　　　　) for eliminating fossil
   fuel use by 2030.

4) 2080 年までに、日本の人口は約 9000 万人まで減少すると見込まれる。

   By 2080, Japan's population is (　　　　　　) to decline to around 90
   million.

★ TRANSLATIONS

日本語に合うように（　　　）の語句を選び替えて、文を完成させなさい。

1) 動物性たんぱく質の多い食事は人々を多くの病気のリスクにさらすとよく言われる。

   It is often said that (a diet / animal fats / at / high / in / people / puts /
   risk of) a number of diseases.

   _____

   _____

2) バターやチーズやアイスクリームは、今日入手可能なごくわずかな乳製品である。

   Butter, cheese, and ice cream are (a / available / few / just / of / products
   / the dairy) today.

   _____

   _____

Magnets for Depression

うつ病は深刻な病気である。薬物やカウンセリングなどの伝統的な治療でも完全に治るというわけではない。脳に刺激を与える新たな治療法がある。

VOCABULARY

下の単語を本文中に探し、(a) ～ (e) の中から語義としてふさわしいものをそれぞれ選びなさい。

1) suicide   2) traditional   3) treatment

4) medication   5) sensation

(a) a way or ways used to help someone recover from a disease
(b) a drug or drugs used to treat disease
(c) a feeling
(d) killing oneself deliberately
(e) following methods from the past

◀)) 1st Listening   まず VOA ニュースを聴きましょう。

SUMMARY CHECK

ニュースの概要として最もふさわしいものを下の 1) ～ 4) のなかから選びなさい。

1) Sonya Kibbee is usually very active.
2) There are no good treatments for depression.
3) Transcranial Magnetic Stimulation is a promising treatment for depression.
4) It is advisable to take pain medication before Transcranial Magnetic Stimulation.

📝 **Notes**

depression: うつ病

Depression is more than just feeling sad. It is a serious disease. Depression can (¹   ) with normal life and a person's sense of self-worth. It can end in suicide.

Some people are helped with traditional treatments, such as medicine or talking with mental health experts. Yet these treatments are not 100 percent (²   ). Luckily, there are other methods people can try.

One such treatment involves bursts of electromagnetic energy. It sends magnetic pulses (³   ) to the brain.

electromagnetic energy: 電極エネルギー
magnetic pulse: 磁気パルス

Sonya Kibbee is from Columbia, Missouri. She works as a physical therapist. Kibbee says she is (⁴   ) active, but because of severe depression last year, she had (⁵   ) making simple decisions.

physical therapist: 理学療法士

"Just dumb little decisions that we make that we don't even think about, I have to think about. And then it just gets me more stressed out because every little decision is hard."

People suffering from depression often seem to (⁶   ) energy or interest in the things around them. Depression affects how much a person (⁷   ) and can interfere with sleep.

Even with medication and talking with mental health professionals, Kibbee said, she (⁸   ) about suicide. Doctors ordered hospital stays for her several times.

Then she heard about TMS, short for Transcranial Magnetic Stimulation. TMS does not involve doctors (⁹   ) on the patient. And the treatment usually does not require anesthesia.

Transcranial Magnetic Stimulation (TMS): 経頭蓋磁気刺激

anesthesia: 麻酔

TMS uses a wire to send powerful magnetic pulses to the brain. During the treatment, (¹⁰   ) feel gentle, repeated beats on their head. The treatment can cause

(^{11}) pain inside the head. So before her treatments, Kibbee took pain medicine, which reduced the sensation. After one week, she said she (^{12}) a real difference.

35   "And I just felt so much better."

After more than 30 treatments, her (^{13}) of depression almost disappeared.

Doctor Muaid Ithman (^{14}) the TMS program at University of Missouri Health Care. He says the treatment

40   can help patients when other methods do not.

"Basically, 50, 60 (^{15}) of people who suffer from treatment resistant depression will see a clinically meaningful response to TMS. And one third of these people will go into remission, which (^{16}) that their

45   symptoms will (^{17}) ... will go away."

The United States National Institute of Mental Health has (^{18}) on two large studies on the safety of TMS. It said they found that most side effects, such as head pain, were minor to moderate. However, the treatment is

50   (^{19}) new. The institute added that long-term side effects are unknown, and more studies are needed.

As for Kibbee, she returned to work and some of her (^{20}) activities.

clinically: 臨床的に

response: 反応

remission: 緩和

symptom: 症状

National Institute of Mental Health: （米国）国立精神保健研究所

side effect: 副作用

minor to moderate: 軽度から中程度の

★ TRUE OR FALSE?

1）～ 5）のなかからニュースの内容として正しいものには T、間違っているものには F を選びなさい。

1) Depression is not a disease.
2) All cases of depression can be cured with medication.
3) Sonya Kibbee is a physical therapist.
4) Depression sometimes interferes with sleep.
5) TMS involves sending powerful magnetic pulses to the brain.

日本語に合うように（　　）を埋めなさい。

1) インターネットの普及にも関わらず、現在、世界の人口のわずか3分の1しかインターネットに接続できない。

    Despite the spread of the internet, currently only one (　　　　　) of the world's population can get online.

2) 致命的ではないが日常活動を行う人間の能力を大いに妨げる病気がたくさんある。

    There are many diseases that are not deadly but greatly (　　　　　) with people's ability to do daily activities.

3) とても多くの課題があるので、あらゆる期限に間に合わせることが困難である。

    I have so many assignments that I'm having (　　　　　) meeting all the deadlines.

4) 多くのアメリカ人はカリウムとマグネシウムのようなミネラルを十分には取っていないと医師たちは言う。

    Doctors say that many Americans are not getting (　　　　　) minerals such as potassium and magnesium.

★ TRANSLATIONS

日本語に合うように（　　）の語句を並び替えて、文を完成させなさい。

1) 日本では、伝統的な漢方薬は従来の西洋医学と並行して存在する。

    In Japan, traditional (alongside / Chinese / conventional / exists / medicine / medicine / western).

    _____

    _____

2) 多くの病は薬なしに自然に治癒すると医師たちが指摘する。

    Doctors point (disorders / many / medication / out / resolve / that / themselves / without).

    _____

    _____

Protect the Reefs!

太平洋上のある国がサンゴ礁の保護のために日焼け止めクリームの廃止を計画している。その計画の背景はどのようなものなのだろうか。

VOCABULARY

下の単語を本文中に探し、(a) ～ (e) の中から語義としてふさわしいものをそれぞれ選びなさい。

1) ban　　　　**2) legislation**　　　**3) statement**

4) waste　　　**5) pollution**

(a) to say officially that something is not allowed
(b) substances that have a harmful effect on the land, water, or air
(c) something said or written officially by an individual or group
(d) unwanted material
(e) a law or set of laws

◀)) 1st Listening　　まず VOA ニュースを聴きましょう。

SUMMARY CHECK

ニュースの概要として最もふさわしいものを下の 1) ～ 4) のなかから選びなさい。

1) Hawaii and Palau are very similar.
2) Palau will soon ban some types of sunscreen.
3) It is important not to scare away tourists.
4) Recent research in Palau suggests that some sunscreens can damage coral reefs.

📝 **Notes**

The Pacific nation of Palau will soon ban many types of sunscreen in an (¹　　　） to protect its coral reefs.

President Tommy Remengesau Jr. (²　　　） legislation recently that bans "reef-toxic" sunscreen beginning in
5　2020. The law defines reef-toxic sunscreen as containing any one of 10 chemicals, (³　　　） oxybenzone. Other chemicals may also be banned.

Officials will take banned sunscreens from (⁴　　　） who carry them into the country. Businesses that sell the
10　banned products will be (⁵　　　） up to $1,000.

In a statement, Remengesau said that the punishments find the right balance between "(⁶　　　） tourists and scaring them away."

The law also (⁷　　　） tour operators to start
15　providing customers with reusable cups, drinking (⁸　　　） and food containers.

The president said the legislation was introduced (⁹　　　） on information from a 2017 report. The report found that sunscreen products were (¹⁰　　　） in Palau's
20　famous Jellyfish Lake. The lake was closed for more than a year because of a (¹¹　　　） in jellyfish numbers. It was recently (¹²　　　）.

The president also noted that plastic waste, chemical pollution and climate change all (¹³　　　） the country's
25　environmental health.

In July, the American state of Hawaii banned the (¹⁴　　　） of sunscreen containing the chemicals oxybenzone and octinoxate beginning in 2021. However, tourists will still be able to bring the banned sunscreen
30　with them into the (¹⁵　　　）. They may also buy the sunscreen in Hawaii if they have a doctor's prescription.

---

coral reef: サンゴ礁

toxic: 有害な

oxybenzone: オキシベンゾン

statement: 声明
punishment: 処罰

scare away: 〜を追い払う

reusable: 再利用可能な

jellyfish: クラゲ

octinoxate: オクチノキサート

prescription: 処方箋

Scientists have found that some chemicals in sunscreen can be toxic to coral reefs. The reefs are an important part of the ocean environment and popular with tourists. But

35 some (¹⁶   ) say there are not enough independent scientific studies on the (¹⁷   ). Others worry that people will suffer from too much sun contact if they stop using the products.

Some manufacturers have already (¹⁸   ) selling

40 "reef-friendly" sunscreen.

Palau is located east of the Philippines and north of Indonesia. The nation is home to 21,000 people. Its economy (¹⁹   ) on tourism and fishing. Palau has an agreement with the United States that provides economic

45 assistance, defense of the territory and other (²⁰   ).

territory: 領土

★ TRUE OR FALSE?

1) ～ 5) のなかからニュースの内容として正しいものには T、間違っているものには F を選びなさい。

1) In Palau, sunscreens containing oxybenzone are considered safe.
2) Visitors will be able to carry banned sunscreen into Palau freely.
3) Sunscreen products have been found in Jellyfish Lake.
4) Hawaii has decided to allow the free sale of sunscreen containing oxybenzone and octinoxate.
5) Palau is located to the west of the Philippines.

日本語に合うように（　　　）を埋めなさい。

1) 日本は中国東方の太平洋に位置する島国である。

Japan is an island nation (　　　　　　　) in the Pacific Ocean to the east of China.

2) イギリス経済は金融サービス業界に大きく依存している。

The British economy depends to a large extent (　　　　　) the financial services industry.

3) インフルエンザに罹っている人たちは十分な休養を取って他の人たちとの接触を避けるべきだ。

People (　　　　　　) from the flu should get plenty of rest and avoid contact with other people.

4) これまで集められた証拠に基づくと、日焼け止め剤に使用されている化学物質の中には環境的に有毒であるものもあるようだ。

Based (　　　　　) the evidence that has been gathered so far, it seems that some chemicals used in sunscreens are environmentally toxic.

日本語に合うように（　　　）の語句を選び替えて、文を完成させなさい。

1) 環境を改善しようとしている各国政府は一般的に経済政策と法律の組み合わせを使う。

Governments (a combination / generally / improve / of / the environment / trying to / use) economic measures and legislation.

_____

_____

2) 危機をどのように対処する緊急会議の後、政府は国民に声明を発表した。

After an emergency meeting (crisis / deal / decide / how / the / to / to / with), the government issued a statement to the public.

_____

_____

Improving Memory in the Aged

高齢者になると記憶力が衰えるが、
その記憶力を高める研究が行われ
ている。どのような研究なのかを
考えてみよう。

VOCABULARY

下の単語を本文中に探し、(a) ～ (e) の中から語義としてふさわしいものをそれぞれ選びなさ
い。

1) brain 　　2) subject 　　3) volunteer

4) method 　　5) worsen

(a) to become less good
(b) the organ in the brain that controls thought
(c) someone who helps with a job without requiring payment
(d) a person who takes part in an experiment
(e) a way of doing something

🔊 1st Listening 　　まず VOA ニュースを聴きましょう。

SUMMARY CHECK

ニュースの概要として最もふさわしいものを下の 1) ～ 4) のなかから選びなさい。

1) The study described in the passage involved young people and old
people.
2) An important study has recently been published in *Nature
Neuroscience*.
3) A study suggests that treating the brains of older people with
electrical charges may improve their memory.
4) Robert Reinhart's work gives us important insights into the nature
and functioning of working memory in healthy people.

📝 **Notes**

A special device (¹   ) on the head that sends electrical charges into the brain may improve the memory abilities of older people. The device may even give them the ability to remember things as well as a person 20 to 30

5　years younger than them.

electrical charge: 電荷
（物体が帯びている静電気
の量）

These are the findings of a study released in the (²   ) publication *Nature Neuroscience* earlier this month.

Nature Neuroscience: 『ネ
イチャー・ニューロサイエン
ス』誌

Researchers working on the study found that the age-

10　related damage to working memory can be (³   ). This is possible, they found, through stimulating two important areas of the brain at a special rhythm.

working memory: 作業記
憶（短い時間に心の中で情
報を保持し、同時に処理す
る能力）

Working memory is the information held (⁴   ) for use in immediate activities such as reasoning and decision-

15　making.

immediate: 即時の
reasoning: 論理的に判断
すること
decision-making: 意思決
定すること

The study (⁵   ) 42 younger adults aged 20 to 29 and 42 older adults aged 60 to 76. The researchers tested all subjects for their (⁶   ) in a working-memory activity.

20　The findings are still early and only (⁷   ) to healthy volunteers. But the findings could point to new ways to increase brain operation in older people suffering from (⁸   ) that affect these operations, such as dementia and Alzheimer's patients.

dementia: 認知症

25　Electroencephalography, or EEG, is a method of (⁹   ) brain activity. Transcranial alternating-current stimulation, or tACS, is the (¹⁰   ) of sending electrical charges into the brain. Using both EEG and tACS, the scientists stimulated the brains of the group of

electroencephalogra-
phy (EEG) 脳波記録法
transcranial alternat-
ing-current stimulation
(tACS): 経頭蓋交流刺激

30　young and old people. They were able to make small changes to the brainwave connections (¹¹   ) to their

stimulate: ～を刺激する

working memory.

Without brain stimulation, the older people were slower and (^{12}) correct in their memories than the
35 younger ones.

This was because the younger people had higher levels of connections of certain brain wave rhythms, the researchers said. This suggests that centering the treatment on these (^{13}) of rhythms in the older
40 people's brains might help their operations.

Robert Reinhart is a researcher at Boston University. He co-led the study. He said that when older adults (^{14}) active brain stimulation, they improved their working-memory test scores to the levels of the younger
45 people. The effect (^{15}) for at least 50 minutes after the stimulation was given.

Reinhart said that the findings open up new (^{16}) for research. But he had no (^{17}) suggestions for the findings' use in medicine.
50 "Much more basic science has to be (^{18}) first," he added.

Neuroscientists agreed that the findings (^{19}) interesting questions about how working memory operates, and how it worsens with age. But they also agree that
55 more research is needed before the treatment can be developed for wider (^{20}).

neuroscientist: 脳神経科学者

★ TRUE OR FALSE?

1) ～ 5) のなかからニュースの内容として正しいものには T、間違っているものには F を選びなさい。

1) Researchers believe it is possible to repair age-related damage to working memory.

2) The number of subjects involved in the research was greater than 80.

3) The technique used to stimulate the brain is called EEG.

4) In general, because of their experiences of life, older people have better working memory than younger people.

5) In the study, brain stimulation led to better working memory performance in older people.

★★21

日本語に合うように（　　　）を埋めなさい。

1) tACS を使っている最近の研究は、私たちが齢を取るにつれて、どのように作業記憶が変化するかに関して興味深い疑問を引き起こしている。

   Recent research using tACS has (　　　　　　　) interesting questions about how working memory changes as we grow older.

2) 認知症にかかっている人たちは、高齢者と若者の脳を比較する研究からいつかは恩恵を受けるだろう。

   People (　　　　　　　) from dementia may eventually benefit from research that compares older people's and younger people's brains.

3) 多くの国々の人たちが急激に高齢化するので、認知症に関係する研究は優先されるべきである。

   With the populations of many countries aging rapidly, dementia- (　　　　　　　) research should be a priority.

4) 基礎医学の研究は、そのうちに治療の新たな可能性を切り開くことになるかもしれない。

   Basic medical research may eventually open up new (　　　　　　　) for treatments.

★ **TRANSLATIONS**

日本語に合うように（　　　）の語句を選び替えて、文を完成させなさい。

1) 革新的な治療なしには、認知症を取り巻く状況は悪化を続けると思える。

   Without innovative treatments, it seems that the (around / continue / dementia / situation / to / will / worsen).

   _____

   _____

2) 多くの環境や政治の運動はボランティアの仕事に頼っている。

   Many environmental and political (depend / movements / of / on / the / volunteers / work).

   _____

   _____

Unit 6

Helping Trees Talk to Us

木々に装着された装置が木々の成長や森林の全体的な状態を測定する。森林を監視している人たちは得られた情報を伐採や植林などに生かす。

VOCABULARY

下の単語を本文中に探し、(a) ～ (e) の中から語義としてふさわしいものをそれぞれ選びなさい。

1) absorb   2) official   3) threat

4) width   5) harvest

(a) to gather crops, wood, etc.
(b) something that could be dangerous
(c) the distance from one side of something to the opposite side
(d) to take in a substance
(e) a person with some authority in an organization

🔊 1st Listening   まず VOA ニュースを聴きましょう。

SUMMARY CHECK

ニュースの概要として最もふさわしいものを下の 1) ～ 4) のなかから選びなさい。

1) A new device attached to trees sends information to forest managers.
2) Forests are more important than originally believed.
3) Riccardo Valentini has become head of the Euro-Mediterranean Center on Climate Change.
4) The amount of carbon dioxide in the atmosphere is increasing rapidly.

📝 **Notes**

A device called a TreeTalker is providing information about trees to people who oversee forests and woodlands. The device (^{1}) to measure the growth and general health of trees. Scientists say the new technology is important because trees are believed to be under increasing (^{2}) because of changes in the world's climate.

Scientists say forests are important because they absorb, or take in, carbon dioxide. It is one of the gases (^{3}) by burning oil and other fossil fuels. Studies show that carbon dioxide is a heat-trapping gas. It has been linked to a general warming in the Earth's (^{4}).

carbon dioxide: 二酸化炭素
fossil fuel: 化石燃料

heat-trapping gas: 温暖化ガス

Antonio Brunori is Secretary-General of PEFC Italy. PEFC is short for the Programme for the Endorsement of Forest Certification. The organization says it works to support good methods for overseeing and developing forest (^{5}).

Programme for the Endorsement of Forest Certification: 森林認証プログラム

Brunori says the world is at a historic period for climate change because the scientific world is on (^{6}). He added that many scientists say, 'Be careful, the ecosystem of the forests is not able anymore, as it was before, to absorb all this carbon dioxide.'

ecosystem: 生態系

Rising temperatures, Brunori noted, are (^{7}) forests under increased stress. He said that harmful insects and diseases are becoming more of a (^{8}) to trees. This is bad for the environment, but also bad for the timber industry.

The TreeTalker devices serve as an early warning system for people overseeing forests. Brunori said TreeTalker turns "eco-physiological signals, such as (^{9}), absorption of carbon dioxide, liquid flow from

eco-physiological: 生態生理学の

roots to leaves, into scientific information." This information can help show if a tree is under (^{10}) from insects or other organisms. The TreeTalker sends its

35 information to forest managers.

organism: 生命体

Riccardo Valentini (^{11}) the new device. He also is head of the Euro-Mediterranean Center on Climate Change. "The TreeTalker device transmits data (^{12}) radio and it can transmit data actually a very

40 long distance, up to one kilometer," Valentini said. The information (^{13}) forestry officials take action immediately to control threats.

Euro-Mediterranean Center on Climate Change: 欧州地中海気象変動センター
transmit: 〜を送る
radio: 無線通信

The TreeTalker is able to measure the width of the (^{14}) of a tree. Timber industry workers can use

45 this information to know how much wood they are growing (^{15}) to how much they are harvesting.

Another (^{16}) is to give scientists the information they need to understand how climate affects forests and the (^{17}) trees play in a healthy environment. "So

50 forests are important, and forests are made by trees. So we need to study the (^{18}) to understand the forest," Valentini added.

About 300 TreeTalker devices are (^{19}) tested in Italy and other countries, such as China and Russia.

55 Valentini (^{20}) another 1,700 devices to be tested worldwide this year.

★ TRUE OR FALSE?

1) 〜 5) のなかからニュースの内容として正しいものには T、間違っているものには F を選びなさい。

1) Forests absorb carbon dioxide.

2) Carbon monoxide is the gas that is most responsible for global warming.

3) These days, more trees are under threat from harmful insects and diseases.

4) The TreeTalker is a device that records information about a tree's health.

5) The TreeTalker can send data up to 100 kilometers.

日本語に合うように（　　　）を埋めなさい。

1) FAO は Food and Agriculture Organization of the United Nations の省略である。

"FAO" is (　　　　　　　　　) for the "Food and Agriculture Organization of the United Nations."

2) すぐに行動が起こされなければ、科学者たちは多くの種が絶滅すると予期している。

If action is not taken soon, scientists (　　　　　　　　) many species to become extinct.

3) どれだけお金を使っているのかと比較してどれだけお金を稼いでいるのかの記録をつけるのが重要である。

It's important to keep track of how much money you are earning (　　　　　　) to how much you are spending.

4) 節約するために、直行便の代わりに、上海経由でバンコクに行った。

To save money, they flew to Bangkok (　　　　　　) Shanghai rather than flying directly.

★ TRANSLATIONS

日本語に合うように（　　　）の語句を並び替えて、文を完成させなさい。

1) さらなる地球の温暖化を防ぐために、植える木よりも切り取る木を少なくすることが重要である。

To prevent further global warming, it is important (fewer / harvest / plant / than / to / trees / we).

_____

_____

2) 気温が上昇していて、森林火災が以前よりも大きな脅威となっている。

With rising temperatures, forest fires (a / are / becoming / before / greater / than / threat).

_____

_____

Unit 7

Healing with Rice

遺伝子組み換えされた穀類の一つがエイズの原因となるウイルスの感染を防ぐ可能性があることがわかった。遺伝子操作は人間の健康に影響はないのか。

■ VOCABULARY

下の単語を本文中に探し、(a) ～ (e) の中から語義としてふさわしいものをそれぞれ選びなさい。

1) virus　　　**2) protein**　　　**3) cure**

4) decade　　　**5) groundbreaking**

(a) a treatment that makes a disease go away
(b) very original or new
(c) ten years
(d) very small organic material that causes disease
(e) a natural substance contained in meat, eggs, and beans

◀)) 1st Listening　　まず VOA ニュースを聴きましょう。

SUMMARY CHECK

ニュースの概要として最もふさわしいものを下の 1) ～ 4) のなかから選びなさい。

1) Infected rice is causing the spread of HIV.
2) A new genetically engineered rice may help block the spread of HIV.
3) The Joint United Nations Program on HIV/AIDS is making progress in understanding HIV.
4) New treatments are urgently required in order to fight HIV/AIDS.

📝 **Notes**

Researchers say a new genetically modified rice can prevent infections of HIV, the virus (^{1}) for the disease AIDS.

genetically modified: 遺伝子組み換えの
infection: 感染

The researchers recently published their findings in a study in the (^{2}) *Proceedings of the National Academy of Sciences*. The team included scientists from America, Britain and Spain.

Proceedings of the National Academy of Sciences (PNAS): プロシーディングズ・オブ・ザ・ナショナル・アカデミー・オブ・サイエンス

The study reports the newly-developed rice produces proteins that attach (^{3}) to the HIV virus. This process prevents the virus from mixing with human cells. The scientists say this can neutralize the virus and (^{4}) its transmission.

neutralize: 〜を中和する

transmission: 伝染

The Joint United Nations Program on HIV/AIDS or UNAIDS reports that worldwide, (^{5}) 37 million people were living with HIV in 2017. The organization says the largest number of (^{6}) were in developing countries. Nearly two-thirds of HIV (^{7}) are in Africa.

Joint United Nations Program on HIV/AIDS(UNAIDS): 国連共同エイズプログラム

There is currently no cure for HIV/AIDS. But there have been major developments in oral drug treatments (^{8}) to slow the progression of the disease. Such treatments can also reduce the chances of (^{9}) the virus on to others. Researchers have also worked on finding a vaccine.

oral: 経口の

UNAIDS says new HIV infections and AIDS-related deaths have been reduced by about 50 percent over the past two decades.

The new study (^{10}) the rice-based method will lead to long-term deployment of the anti-HIV treatment across the developing world. Researchers said the "groundbreaking" (^{11}) is "realistically the only

way" that anti-HIV combination treatments can be
produced at a cost low (^{12}　　　) for the developing
world.

combination treatment: 併用治療

35　The scientists say the (^{13}　　　) and most cost-
effective way to use the rice will be to make it into a cream
to be put on the skin. The HIV-fighting proteins can then
enter the body (^{14}　　　) the skin.

cost-effective: 費用対効果の高い

People in all parts of the world could grow the rice and
40　make the cream themselves, the researchers said. This
would prevent the cost and travel required for many
patients to receive treatments and medicine, (^{15}　　　)
in the developing world.

The scientific team says (^{16}　　　) testing is needed to
45　make sure the genetic engineering process does not
produce any additional chemicals that could be (^{17}　　　)
to people.

genetic engineering: 遺伝子工学

The process of changing the genetic structure of food
crops has been (^{18}　　　) for some time. Such foods are
50　commonly called GMOs — for genetically modified
organisms, or GEs — (^{19}　　　) genetically edited.
Critics of genetically engineered crops believe they can
(^{20}　　　) people.

★ TRUE OR FALSE?

1) ～ 5) のなかからニュースの内容として正しいものには T、間違っているものには F を選びなさい。

1) Scientists from America, Britain, and Spain worked together to develop the genetically modified rice described in the passage.
2) The modified rice can block the transmission of HIV.
3) New HIV infections and AIDS-related deaths are increasing rapidly.
4) The new modified rice can be made into a cream.
5) It has been proved that the new modified rice is safe.

日本語に合うように（　　　）を埋めなさい。

1) 海外旅行に出発する前に、必ずパスポートを持っていなさい。

Before leaving on an overseas trip, (　　　　　　) sure you have your passport with you.

2) これまでかなりの間、この課題に取り組んできたが、あまり進んでいない。

I've been working on this assignment for some (　　　　　　) now, but I'm not making much progress.

3) 日本の GDP（国民総生産）は 2018 年には約 0.8％増加したと算出されている。

Japan's GDP is calculated to have increased (　　　　　　) about 0.8% in 2018.

4) 勉強にもっと多くの時間を費やせば普通もっと良い成績になる。

Spending more time on your studies usually (　　　　　　) to better grades.

★ TRANSLATIONS

日本語に合うように（　　　）の語句を並び替えて、文を完成させなさい。

1) タンパク質は健康的な食事に関するガイド本に書かれている 5 つの食品群の 1 つである。

Proteins constitute (described / eating / food groups / in guides / one of / the five / to healthy).

_____

_____

2) 2010 年代は政治経済の不安定さを特徴としている。

The second (been / by / decade / has / marked / of / the 21st century) political and economic instability.

_____

_____

Unit 8

Helping the Gorillas

アフリカのマウンテンゴリラの生息個体数は長年減少してきていたが、現在ではその数が上昇傾向にある。何が起こっているのだろう。

VOCABULARY

下の単語を本文中に探し、(a) ～ (e) の中から語義としてふさわしいものをそれぞれ選びなさい。

1) illegal 2) unrest 3) endangered

4) cooperate 5) treat

(a) against the law
(b) to try to cure or alleviate disease
(c) to work together
(d) in a state of danger
(e) an unstable state or state of conflict

🔊 1st Listening まず VOA ニュースを聴きましょう。

SUMMARY CHECK

ニュースの概要として最もふさわしいものを下の 1) ～ 4) のなかから選びなさい。

1) After a long period of decline, the mountain gorilla population in Africa is rising.
2) The mountain gorilla is critically endangered.
3) Mountain gorillas risk disappearing from the Democratic Republic of the Congo and neighboring countries.
4) The mountain gorilla is safe.

📝 **Notes**

　　Africa's mountain gorilla population has been (¹　　　　)
for many years. But now, wildlife groups say their numbers
are finally (²　　　　).

population: 生息個体数

　　The mountain gorillas live in protected forest areas in
5　Rwanda, Uganda and the Democratic Republic of the
Congo. But they have faced the danger of disappearing as
their population steadily (³　　　　).

protected forest area:
森林保護地区

　　The gorillas' environment has been threatened by
human agriculture production in (⁴　　　　) areas. Other
10　threats include illegal hunting, civil unrest and human-
introduced diseases.

civil unrest: 社会不安

　　The mountain gorilla had (⁵　　　　) included on an
endangered "Red List" published by the International
Union for Conservation of Nature, or IUCN. It was
15　(⁶　　　　) as "critically endangered." On November 14th,
the Switzerland-based group changed that listing to
"endangered."

endangered: 絶滅危惧 IB
類の（第 4 位）
**International Union for
Conservation of Nature
(IUCN)**: 国際自然保護連合
critically endangered:
絶滅危惧 IA 類の（IUCN
が定めた絶滅危惧種 8 カテ
ゴリの第 3 位）

　　In 2008, the mountain gorilla population was estimated
to be around 680. In 2018, IUCN estimates (⁷　　　　) the
20　number had increased to more than 1,000.

　　IUCN officials noted the new (⁸　　　　) was fueled by
increased and improved conservation programs. Several
nations had cooperated to create effective conservation
(⁹　　　　), the organization said in a statement. This
25　(¹⁰　　　　) to "positive engagement from communities
living around the mountain gorilla habitat," the statement
said.

habitat: 生息地

　　Tara Stoinski is president and chief scientist of the Dian
Fossey Gorilla Fund. The not-for-profit group is (¹¹　　　　)
30　in Atlanta, Georgia. It is named after the researcher
(¹²　　　　) work helped bring international attention to

**Dian Fossey Gorilla
Fund**: ダイアン・フォッシー・
ゴリラ基金
not-for-profit: 非営利的な

mountain gorillas. The organization has been (^{13})
in conservation programs.

35   Stoinski called the IUCN findings a great "conservation success." In a statement, she said mountain gorillas have (^{14}) some of the highest levels of protection of any animal in history. "This is the type of extreme conservation (^{15}) if we want to ensure a future for wildlife," she added.

40   The conservation efforts included increased enforcement measures against illegal hunting and emergency health care for (^{16}) gorillas, the IUCN said.

    One not-for-profit group called Gorilla Doctors keeps medical workers in each of the countries where mountain 45 gorillas live. They are called to treat animals with disease or carry out rescues when gorillas are (^{17}) in traps set for other animals.

    The IUCN also (^{18}) that populations of the threatened fin whale are also on the rise. The group said 50 bans on commercial whaling in the North Pacific Ocean and (^{19}) had helped some of the populations grow. The fin whale appeared on the Red List as "endangered," but that has been (^{20}) to "vulnerable."

Glossary (right margin):
effort: 取り組み
enforcement measures: 強制措置
emergency: 緊急事態

trap: わな

fin whale: ナガスクジラ
on the rise: 上昇中で
ban: 禁止

vulnerable: 絶滅危惧II類の（第5位）

★ TRUE OR FALSE?

1) ～ 5) のなかからニュースの内容として正しいものには T、間違っているものには F を選びなさい。

1) The mountain gorilla has disappeared from Uganda.

2) Illegal hunting has never been a problem for the mountain gorilla.

3) The mountain gorilla is classified as "endangered."

4) The Dian Fossey Gorilla Fund is a for-profit group.

5) Tara Stoinski believes that the measures taken to protect mountain gorillas were largely unnecessary.

日本語に合うように ( ) を埋めなさい。

1) 新たな保護の取り組みが、マウンテンゴリラの保護プログラムの成功によって活気づけられることになるのを科学者たちが望んでいる。

Scientists hope that new conservation efforts will be ( ) by the success of mountain gorilla conservation programs.

2) 2018 年のマウンテンゴリラの生息個体数は 1 千頭以上であると推定されている。

The mountain gorilla population in 2018 was ( ) to be over 1,000.

3) 多くの動物種は生息地の喪失にひどく脅かされている。

Many animal species are severely ( ) by habitat loss.

4) マウンテンゴリラは人間にもたらされた病気に感染する危険性に直面している。

Mountain gorillas ( ) the danger of catching diseases introduced by humans.

★ **TRANSLATIONS** ░░░░

日本語に合うように ( ) の語句を並び替えて、文を完成させなさい。

1) 絶滅の危機に瀕した動植物種の数は容赦なく増加を続けている。

The number (animal and plant / continues / endangered / of / rise / species / to) inexorably.

_____

_____

2) 環境政策の実施は社会不安のある地域ではとても困難である。

Implementation of environmental policies (areas / civil / difficult in / is / of / unrest / very).

_____

_____

No More Misinformation!

ワクチンに関する誤解や誤報がインターネット上で広がっているが、これは止められるべきであると国際的な団体の代表者が言う。その真相は何か。

VOCABULARY

下の単語を本文中に探し、(a) ～ (e) の中から語義としてふさわしいものをそれぞれ選びなさい。

1) misinformation   2) measles   3) confuse

4) strengthen   5) delegate

(a) to make someone feel as if they do not understand
(b) incorrect information
(c) to make stronger
(d) a representative of a group at a meeting
(e) an infectious disease with a fever and red spots on the face

◀)) 1st Listening   まず VOA ニュースを聴きましょう。

SUMMARY CHECK

ニュースの概要として最もふさわしいものを下の 1) ～ 4) のなかから選びなさい。

1) Recently, there is a lot of misinformation on the internet.
2) Seth Berkley has recently become the president of Gavi, the Vaccine Alliance.
3) Officials warn that misinformation on the internet about vaccines is highly dangerous and should be stopped.
4) The U.S. supports many vaccination programs around the world.

📝 **Notes**

The head of an international vaccine group says that misunderstandings and false information about vaccines are (¹　　　) on the internet and should be stopped.

Seth Berkley of Gavi, the Vaccine Alliance, spoke
5　Tuesday to a (²　　　) in Geneva, Switzerland, where the World Health Organization is meeting. Berkley said that false information "kills people." He noted strong scientific (³　　　) of the safety of vaccines.

But, he said, social media algorithms favor
10　misinformation over (⁴　　　). He added that such misinformation easily influences people who have not had a family member die from a (⁵　　　) disease.

Berkley said people must consider the belief in misinformation as a contagious sickness.

15　He added, "This is a disease. This (⁶　　　) at the speed of light, literally."

The World Health Organization says not enough people are getting the vaccine that prevents measles. It says this is (⁷　　　) the disease is spreading around the world.

20　The organization says vaccines save two million (⁸　　　) every year.

Measles infections have (⁹　　　) sharply in countries that earlier had few cases, including the United States.

Seth Berkley argues that misinformation about vaccines
25　is not a (¹⁰　　　) of speech issue. He said Tuesday that social media companies should remove such content from their websites.

Alex Azar is Secretary of the U.S. Department of Health and Human Services. He made (¹¹　　　) comments in
30　his speech to the yearly meeting of the WHO. He said in the U.S., social media conspiracy groups confuse parents

Notes (margin):

Gavi (Global Alliance for Vaccine and Immunization): 世界ワクチン予防接種同盟
World Health Organization (WHO): 世界保健機構

algorithm: アルゴリズム（数学的な問題を解くための一連の手順）

contagious: 人から人への接触によって直接感染する

literally: 文字通り

case: 症例

secretary: 長官
Department of Health and Human Services: 保健社会福祉省

conspiracy: 陰謀

so they (¹²   ) getting needed vaccinations.

The American official also spoke of U.S. efforts to strengthen immunization programs around the world. He
35 said, "Just recently, the U.S. supported a mass measles vaccination (¹³   ) in Nigeria that reached almost 10 million kids. We assisted with a diphtheria outbreak among Rohingya refugees in Bangladesh."

diphtheria: ジフテリア
outbreak: 大流行
refugee: 難民

And he noted U.S. support of (¹⁴   ) research about
40 the yellow fever vaccine.

yellow fever: 黄熱病

Azar has (¹⁵   ) criticism of comments about vaccines made by U.S. president Donald Trump before he became president. Trump (¹⁶   ) on Twitter that vaccination could cause autism, a developmental disorder.

criticism: 批判

autism: 自閉症

45 He wrote in 2012:

"A study says @Autism is out of (¹⁷   ) — a 78% increase in 10 years. Stop giving monstrous combined vaccinations."

monstrous: 怪物のような

Azar said that Trump was "extremely firm" in
50 (¹⁸   ) of vaccinations.

firm: 強硬な

Canada's Chief Public Health Officer Theresa Tam also (¹⁹   ) to the WHO delegates. She said health officials needed to do more about (²⁰   ) misinformation. She said she was working on the issue
55 with Twitter, Facebook, Google and other companies.

Chief Public Health
Officer: 最高公衆衛生責任
者

★ TRUE OR FALSE?

1) ～ 5) のなかからニュースの内容として正しいものには T、間違っているものには F を選びなさい。

1) Seth Berkley thinks that evidence for the safety of vaccines is weak.

2) Seth Berkley thinks that believing in medical misinformation is a kind of disease.

3) Measles is spreading around the world because not enough people are being vaccinated against it.

4) In the passage, an official mentions a measles vaccination campaign in Bangladesh.

5) Theresa Tam is a U.S. government official.

USEFUL EXPRESSIONS

日本語に合うように ( ) を埋めなさい。

1) 国際的な医療グループの代表者が、インターネット上の偽情報を信じる危険性のことを話している。

Representatives of an international medical group have been speaking ( ) the dangers of believing misinformation on the Internet.

2) 各国政府はワクチン接種の問題について非政府機関と連携する必要がある。

Governments need to work with NGOs ( ) the issue of vaccinations.

3) 不十分な公衆衛生対策が、予防しうる病気が原因による人々の死をもたす可能性がある。

Inadequate public health measures can lead to people dying ( ) preventable diseases.

4) ソーシャル・メディア・サイトの偽情報はいささか収拾がつかないと多くの人たちが認めている。

Many people consider that misinformation on social media sites is ( ) of control.

★ TRANSLATIONS

日本語に合うように ( ) の語句を並び替えて、文を完成させなさい。

1) インターネット上の偽情報は医療情報に関してだけでなく政治運動に関しても問題でもある。

Misinformation on the internet is (a problem / also in / but / connection / only as / medical information / not / regards) with political campaigning.

_____

_____

2) 各国政府はソーシャル・メディア・サイトの規制を強化すべきだと多くの解説者たちは言う。

Many commentators (governments / of / regulation / say / should / strengthen / that) social media sites.

_____

_____

No More Mountain Birds?

ペルーの山腹に生息する鳥類がより高いところへ移動し、より小さくなっていることがわかった。その原因は何なのか。

■ VOCABULARY

下の単語を本文中に探し、(a) 〜 (e) の中から語義としてふさわしいものをそれぞれ選びなさい。

1) decrease　　2) elevation　　3) temperature
4) document　　5) prove

(a) to show that something is true
(b) a measure of heat
(c) to record details of something
(d) to become less in quantity, size, etc.
(e) a measure of height or altitude

🔊) 1st Listening　　まず VOA ニュースを聴きましょう。

SUMMARY CHECK

ニュースの概要として最もふさわしいものを下の 1) 〜 4) のなかから選びなさい。

1) John Fitzpatrick and Benjamin Freeman have revolutionized the study of birds in Peru.
2) Two studies of birds in Peru have shown that changes in their environment have led birds to move higher up a mountain, with harmful consequences.
3) A mountain in Peru used to have around 400 species of bird.
4) It took John Fitzpatrick more than 30 years to get his work published in the *Proceedings of the National Academy of Sciences*.

📝 **Notes**

　Scientists have (^{1}　　　) a 1985 study of birds in Peru that shows climate change is (^{2}　　　) them from their natural environment.

　Thirty years ago, researchers studied more than 400 kinds of birds living on a mountainside in Peru. In 2017, researchers looked again at the bird populations. They found that almost all had moved to higher places in the mountain. Almost all had decreased in size. And the scientists say at least eight bird groups that started at the higher elevations had (^{3}　　　) out completely.

population: 個体数

　John W. Fitzpatrick is director of the Cornell Laboratory of Ornithology and a co-writer of the study. He said, "Once you move up as far as you can go, there's nowhere else (^{4}　　　)." The researchers say the birds might have moved up the mountain because of temperature changes. Or, they say, changes to food sources may have (^{5}　　　) them to go higher.

Cornell Laboratory of Ornithology: コーネル大学鳥類学研究所

　The (^{6}　　　) were published in the *Proceedings of the National Academy of Sciences*.

Proceedings of the National Academy of Sciences: 米国科学アカデミー紀要

　Past research has documented birds and other animals moving up in elevation in (^{7}　　　) to warming temperatures. Mark Urban is director of the Center of Biological Risk at the University of Connecticut. He said this (^{8}　　　) study was the first to prove that rising temperatures and moving to avoid them can (^{9}　　　) to extinction.

Center of Biological Risk: センター・オブ・バイオロジカル・リスク

extinction: 絶滅

　In 1985, Fitzpatrick and a team of scientists (^{10}　　　) a camp alongside a river running down a mountainside in southeastern Peru. He wanted to document where tropical bird groups there (^{11}　　　). His team spent several weeks using nets to catch and (^{12}　　　) birds. They kept

tropical: 熱帯の

detailed notes of birds they caught, saw or (^{13}).

detailed: 詳細な

In 2016, Fitzpatrick passed his notes, (^{14}) and other records to Benjamin Freeman. He is with the
35 Biodiversity Research Centre at the University of British Columbia. Freeman has been (^{15}) tropical birds for more than 10 years. He set out in August and September of 2017 to copy Fitzpatrick's study. His team used the same methods, searching the same places in the same time of
40 year.

Biodiversity Research Centre: バイオダイバーシティ・リサーチ・センター

Freeman's team wanted to see how things had changed for the bird groups since 1985. The average temperatures on the mountain had risen 0.42 (^{16}) Celsius.

Celsius: 摂氏（°C）

Freeman's team placed 20 sound recording devices on
45 the mountain to record the sounds of birds that might not (^{17}) be seen. Freeman said that the birds moved an average of 98 meters (^{18}) up the mountain. He said he believes that temperature is the main cause of the birds' movement.

50 Fitzpatrick noted that birds (^{19}) to living in areas with little temperature change may be especially at risk because of climate change. He said, "We should expect that what's happening on this mountain top is happening more (^{20}) in the Andes, and other tropical
55 mountain ranges."

the Andes: アンデス山脈

mountain range: 山脈

★ TRUE OR FALSE?

1)～5) のなかからニュースの内容として正しいものには T、間違っているものには F を選びなさい。

1) Benjamin Freeman's research sought to replicate John Fitzpatrick's research, more than thirty years later.

2) Benjamin Freeman works at the Cornell Laboratory of Ornithology.

3) Between 1985 and 2017, average temperatures on the mountain appear to have risen.

4) Birds that moved up the mountain do not seem to have experienced any harmful effects.

5) Sound recording devices were placed on the mountain.

日本語に合うように (　　　) を埋めなさい。

1) 動物たちは、気温の変化やその他の環境の変化に反応して、移動することがある。

Animals sometimes move in (　　　　　　　) to changing temperatures or other changes in their environment.

2) 鳥たちのなかには、食糧不足によって、住んでいる山のますます高い所へ移動されられているものもいる可能性がある。

It is possible that some birds are being (　　　　　　　) by a lack of food higher and higher up the mountains where they live.

3) 低温に慣れている動物たちは地球温暖化に適応するのが難しいだろう。

Animals (　　　　　　　) to cool temperatures will have difficulty adapting to global warming.

4) ペルーアンデス山脈では、冬の数カ月間の日中の最高と最低の気温が平均で19℃違う。

In the Peruvian Andes, daily high and low temperatures in the winter months differ by an (　　　　　　) of 19℃.

★ TRANSLATIONS

日本語に合うように (　　　) の語句を並び替えて、文を完成させなさい。

1) 化石燃料の使用が劇的に減少すれば、地球温暖化のペースを落とすことは可能かもしれない。

If (decreases / drastically / fossil / fuels / of / use), it may be possible to slow down global warming.

_____

_____

2) 地球温暖化が人間の活動によって引き起こされることを、科学者たちはまだ何の疑いの余地もなく証明していない。

Scientists (all / are / beyond / doubt / prove / to / yet) that global warming is caused by human activity.

_____

_____

Unit 11

The Growing Problem of Dementia

老化は普通のことであるが、認知症は病気であるとWHOは定義している。WHOは認知症予防対策に新たな指針を発表して啓蒙活動を行なっている。

■ VOCABULARY

下の単語を本文中に探し、(a) ～ (e) の中から語義としてふさわしいものをそれぞれ選びなさい。

1) decline   2) rapidly   3) triple

4) evidence   5) adjustment

(a) a drop or decrease
(b) to increase threefold
(c) reasons for believing something is true
(d) quickly
(e) a change made in response to changing circumstances

◀)) 1st Listening   まず VOA ニュースを聴きましょう。

SUMMARY CHECK

ニュースの概要として最もふさわしいものを下の 1) ～ 4) のなかから選びなさい。

1) The WHO has managed to agree on a definition of dementia.
2) People at risk of dementia should take fish oil.
3) 2030 is the year when the dementia crisis is predicted to become unmanageable.
4) The WHO has launched an awareness campaign on dementia.

📝 **Notes**

Aging is normal. But dementia is not a normal part of aging.

The World Health Organization (¹   ) dementia as an illness marked by a decline in a person's ability to think, reason and understand "(²   ) what might be expected from normal aging." It results from a variety of diseases and (³   ) that affect the brain, such as Alzheimer's disease or stroke. About 50 million people around the world have dementia.

WHO experts warn that dementia is a "rapidly growing public health problem." People with dementia are often not able to care for themselves. Their need for care, the WHO (⁴   ), creates great economic problems for families and (⁵   ). Experts estimate that by the year 2030 caring for people with dementia will cost about $2 (⁶   ) every year.

That is (⁷   ) health experts from the World Health Organization said in a recent statement to the press. They add that there are nearly 10 million new cases every year and that number is (⁸   ) to triple by the year 2050.

As a part of their awareness campaign, the WHO released new guidelines for reducing the (⁹   ) of getting dementia. WHO experts say that scientific evidence (¹⁰   ) that what is good for our hearts is also good for our brains. Having an active and healthy lifestyle is the best way to avoid getting dementia as we age.

The WHO guidelines include the following: exercise (¹¹   ); do not smoke; do not drink harmful amounts of alcohol; keep a healthy (¹²   ); eat a healthy diet; keep your blood pressure, cholesterol and blood sugar at healthy levels.

marked by: 〜を特徴とする
reason: 論理的に判断する

a variety of: 様々な〜

Alzheimer disease: アルツハイマー病
stroke: 脳卒中

public health: 公衆衛生

statement: 声明
press: 報道機関

awareness campaign: 啓蒙活動

The guidelines are common (^{13}) advice given by many other health organizations, such as the U.S. National Institute on Aging. But they are important reminders.

35 They can help healthcare providers (^{14}) their patients on what they can do to help prevent cognitive decline and dementia.

The new guidelines can also help governments and policy-makers (^{15}) social programs to help people

40 (^{16}) healthy lifestyles. WHO experts add that possibly following a Mediterranean-style diet may help prevent dementia. But they warn (^{17}) taking vitamin B or E pills, fish oil or other so-called "brain health" pills. They say there is "strong research showing

45 they don't work."

The WHO also advises countries to create support plans to help (^{18}).

Dr. Dévora Kestel is Director of the Department of Mental Health and Substance Abuse at the World Health

50 Organization. In a statement to the press, she said that people who care for people with dementia are very often family members. These family members "need to make (^{19}) adjustments to their family and professional lives to care for their (^{20}) ones."

U.S. National Institute on Aging: アメリカ国立老化研究所
reminder: 思い出させるもの [ヒント]

cognitive: 認知作用の

pill: 錠剤

Department of Mental Health and Substance Abuse: 精神衛生・薬物乱用部門局

adjustment: 調整

⭐ TRUE OR FALSE?

1)～5) のなかからニュースの内容として正しいものには T、間違っているものには F を選びなさい。

1) About 500,000 people around the world have dementia.

2) It is estimated that the cost of caring for people with dementia will reach about $2,000,000,000,000.

3) Advice given to avoid dementia is generally incompatible with that given to avoid heart disease.

4) Vitamin E supplements are recommended for those at risk of dementia.

5) A Mediterranean diet is often considered to be healthy.

★ USEFUL EXPRESSIONS

日本語に合うように (　　　) を埋めなさい。

1) 患者に投薬するだけではなく、病気を予防するために何ができるかを助言するのも、医師には重要である。

It is important for doctors not only to give their patients medicine but also to advise them on (　　　　　　　) they can do to avoid disease.

2) 医療専門家は酒を大量に飲むことと喫煙しないように強く警告する。

Medical experts warn strongly (　　　　　　　) drinking heavily and smoking.

3) 脳卒中は血流の欠乏によって引き起こされる脳細胞の死と通常は定義される。

A stroke is usually (　　　　　　　) as the death of brain cells caused by a loss of blood flow.

4) 健康な老年期のために、体重の増やしすぎを避けるのが望ましい。

For a healthy old age, it is advisable to (　　　　　　　) gaining too much weight.

★ TRANSLATIONS

日本語に合うように (　　　) の語句を並び替えて、文を完成させなさい。

1) 医療専門家によると、たいていの栄養補助食品の有効性にはほとんど証拠がない。

According to medical experts, there (evidence / for / is / little / most / of / supplements / the effectiveness).

_____

_____

2) 多くの人は野菜の摂取量を少なくとも３倍にすべきだと栄養士たちは言う。

Nutritionists say that many people (intake / least / of / should at / their / triple / vegetables).

_____

_____

Student Walkouts

ベルギーやヨーロッパ各国の生徒たちが学校を欠席して抗議活動に参加している。彼らは気象変動と闘うための行動を社会に求めている。

VOCABULARY

下の単語を本文中に探し、(a) ～ (e) の中から語義としてふさわしいものをそれぞれ選びなさい。

1) protest   2) skip   3) presence
4) mature   5) coal

(a) able to make reasonable decisions, like an adult
(b) a black material that can be burned as fuel
(c) to be somewhere, not to be absent
(d) to not attend something that you should
(e) an event where people show they disagree with something

◀)) 1st Listening   まず VOA ニュースを聴きましょう。

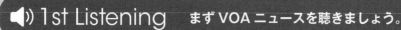

SUMMARY CHECK

ニュースの概要として最もふさわしいものを下の 1) ～ 4) のなかから選びなさい。

1) The Belgian government is getting increasingly worried about climate change.
2) These days, many political movements start in Sweden.
3) It is important to join demonstrations even if the weather is bad.
4) Students in Brussels and other European countries have been joining demonstrations hoping for action against climate change.

📝 **Notes**

Thousands of Belgian students (¹   ) away from school the past two Thursdays to join protests in Brussels. The protesters have been (²   ) action to fight climate change.

protest: 抗議行動

5　The first demonstration took place on January 10. Organizers have (³   ) plans to keep holding demonstrations every Thursday. Many students have promised to skip classes and join the protesters.

demonstration: デモ、示威行動

About 3,000 Belgian students attended the first protest, 10 (⁴   ) Youth for Climate, the *Brussels Times* reported. More than 10,000 students joined the second demonstration, (⁵   ) on January 17. The number included young people from both the country's Flemish-speaking north and French-speaking south.

Youth for Climate: ユース・フォー・クライミット
Brussels Times: 『ブリュッセル・タイムズ』紙

Flemish-speaking: フランドル語を話す

15　That day, protesters (⁶   ) cold and wet weather conditions in Brussels. They carried (⁷   ) with messages like "School strike 4 Climate" and "Skipping school? No. We fight for our future." The demonstrations were peaceful, with no (⁸   ) reported.

20　More than 75,000 people took to the streets of Brussels last month in Belgium's largest-ever climate (⁹   ). But the latest protests were held especially for school-aged students who chose to miss class.

The student protesters have demanded stronger 25 government environment policies (¹⁰   ) to climate change.

Before the first protest, school officials warned students that missing school — even to attend a demonstration — (¹¹   ) school and government policies.

30　But before the second protest, many schools decided to give students (¹²   ) to take part, the *Brussels Times*

reported. The newspaper said students would (^{13})
asked to prove their presence by showing a picture of
themselves at the protest.

35   Patrick Lancksweerdt is the director of one school. He
told *De Standaard* newspaper that "education has to turn
youngsters into mature (^{14}). By their actions, they
proved that they are."

De Standaard: 『ドゥ・スタ
ンダード』紙

The European Environmental Bureau, or EEB, has
40   (^{15}) support for the student marches. The EEB is a
collection of environmental activist groups across Europe.
It has (^{16}) European leaders to support action to
reduce (^{17}) on coal, oil and natural gas.

European Environmen-
tal Bureau (EEB): 欧州環
境団体事務所
march: 行進
environmental activist:
環境活動家

The EEB says the idea for "school strike" movements
45   centered on the Earth's environment came from Swedish
student activist Greta Thunberg. She received (^{18})
for skipping school one day a week so that she could
demonstrate in front of Sweden's parliament building.

parliament: 議会

The movement started in Sweden (^{19}) to be
50   growing. On January 18th, thousands of students in
Germany and Switzerland (^{20}) to skip class to
press for more action against climate change.

★ TRUE OR FALSE?

1) ～ 5) のなかからニュースの内容として正しいものには T、間違っているものには F を選びなさい。

1) Students' aim in protesting was to get stronger action against climate
change.

2) At the beginning, many schools advised students not to miss school to
join the demonstrations.

3) In a newspaper, Patrick Lancksweerdt strongly opposed students'
participation in protests.

4) The European Environmental Bureau is an official governmental
organization.

5) Greta Thurnberg is a student activist from Belgium.

日本語に合うように (　　　) を埋めなさい。

1) 学生たちは、各国政府が気象変動の危機を真摯に受け止めるよう促している。

   Students have been (　　　　　　　　) governments to take the threat of climate change seriously.

2) できることはどんなやり方でも地球温暖化に対して私たち皆が行動をおこすことは重要である。

   It is important that we all take action (　　　　　　　　) global warming in whatever ways we can.

3) 化石燃料への過度の依存は多くの環境問題の原因となる。

   Excessive (　　　　　　　) on fossil fuels leads to many environmental problems.

4) 学校は、重要な行事に参加するために授業を休む許可を学生に与えることがある。

   Schools sometimes give students (　　　　　　　　) to miss classes in order to take part in important events.

日本語に合うように (　　　) の語句を並び替えて、文を完成させなさい。

1) 食事を抜くことは体重を減らすのに良い方法ではないということにほとんどの医者が同意する。

   Most doctors agree that (good / is / lose / meals / not a / skipping / way to) weight.

   _____

   _____

2) 数カ国に、次の10年間で燃料として石炭を使うすべての発電所を段階的に廃棄する計画がある。

   In several countries, there are (all power / as / fuel over / out / phase / plans to / stations / using coal) the next decade.

   _____

   _____

Unit 13

Immigrants in Health Care

アメリカへの移住を制限する案が
出されているが、老人や障害者の
世話をする労働者の国家的な不足
をもたらすことが危惧されている。

VOCABULARY

下の単語を本文中に探し、(a) ～ (e) の中から語義としてふさわしいものをそれぞれ選びなさ
い。

1) shortage   2) immigrant   3) disorder
4) aide   5) double

(a) someone who enters a country to live there
(b) a situation where there is not enough of something
(c) a person whose job is to assist someone
(d) an illness
(e) to increase two-fold

◄») 1st Listening   まず VOA ニュースを聴きましょう。

SUMMARY CHECK

ニュースの概要として最もふさわしいものを下の 1) ～ 4) のなかから選びなさい。

1) Proposed changes to immigration policy in the U.S. may make it difficult to find enough workers to care for disabled and old people.
2) The U.S. healthcare system employs more than three million immigrants.
3) Doctor Leah Zallman, a professor of medicine at Harvard Medical School, has recently written an important report on immigration.
4) People in "direct care work" include nurses.

📝 **Notes**

Proposed limits on immigration to the United States may (¹   ) the nation's shortage of workers who care for old and disabled people, a new study finds.

More than three million immigrants work within the
5　U.S. healthcare system. That (²   ) 18 percent of all health care workers. Nearly 25 percent of care providers in nursing homes nationwide are immigrants. Nursing homes care for elderly adults and people with a physical disability or long-term health disorder.

10　Doctor Leah Zallman is a professor of medicine at Harvard Medical School in Massachusetts. She was the (³   ) writer of a report on the study. The report appeared (⁴   ) this month in the publication *Health Affairs*.

Zallman said, "We rely heavily on immigrants to care for
15　the elderly and disabled, (⁵   ) in their everyday care."

To take a (⁶   ) look at the importance of immigrants in the healthcare system, Zallman and other researchers examined the *Annual Social and Economic Supplement* of the *2018 Current Population Survey*.

20　The survey found that 1 million workers in the long-term healthcare industry were immigrants. That represents 23.5 percent of total workers in such jobs. Zallman noted that immigrants are (⁷   ) likely to work overnight hours. "This is an industry that needs people round-the-
25　clock," she said. "They are really (⁸   ) the gaps."

In 2017, more than 27 percent of direct care workers were immigrants. The study (⁹   ) "direct care work" as nurses, home health aides or home care aides. Such workers help with everyday activities like helping
30　people eat meals, put on (¹⁰   ) and wash up.

Nurses and health aides perform other (¹¹   ),

Notes (margin):

healthcare system: 医療制度
care worker: 介護福祉士

nursing home: 老人ホーム
physical disability: 身体障害

Health Affairs:『ヘルス・アフアーズ』誌

Annual Social and Economic Supplement:『年次社会経済補足』
2018 Current Population Survey:『2018 年人口動態調査』

round-the-clock: 24 時間対応の

wash up: 手や顔を洗う

such as taking a patient's blood pressure and offering range-of-motion exercises.

range-of-motion exercise: 関節可動域訓練

35 Home care aides may help clean a patient's home and cook food for them. They do not perform medical tasks.

medical task: 医療行為

The elderly population in America is (^{12}) to double by the year 2050. Workers who are prepared to care for elderly or disabled patients are already in short (^{13}), the researchers noted. The Health Resources

Health Resources and Services Administration: 保健資源事業局

40 and Services Administration predicts a 34-percent (^{14}) in the demand for direct care workers over the next 10 years.

Last month, the administration of President Donald

administration: 政権

Trump (^{15}) legislation that would reduce the

45 number of legal immigrants while placing more importance on educated, (^{16}) immigrants. Such changes, the report noted, "could (^{17}) reduce the number of low-wage immigrant workers."

Albert Wu is a doctor and (^{18}) of health policy

50 at the Johns Hopkins School of Public Health in Maryland.

Johns Hopkins School of Public Health: ジョーンズ・ホプキンス公衆衛生大学院

He called the new study "very important and timely."

Wu said, "The current (^{19}) to restrict immigration to more skilled or professional applicants

applicant: 応募者

(^{20}) directly counter to the need for this category

category: 種類

55 of work."

★ TRUE OR FALSE?

1) ～ 5) のなかからニュースの内容として正しいものには T、間違っているものには F を選びなさい。

1) The majority of care providers in nursing homes in the U.S. are immigrants.

2) Typically, a home care aide will do things like taking a patient's blood pressure.

3) It is predicted that the elderly population in the U.S. will triple by 2050.

4) Proposed legislation may reduce the number of low-wage immigrant workers.

5) Albert Wu works at Harvard Medical School.

★ USEFUL EXPRESSIONS

日本語に合うように (   ) を埋めなさい。

1) 経済成長を目的とする多くの政策は環境保護の必要と矛盾する。

Many policies aimed at economic growth run (   ) to the need to protect the environment.

2) 国民のための無料あるいは低負担の医療の提供を特に重視する国もある。

Some countries place a great (   ) of importance on providing free or low-cost healthcare for citizens.

3) 多くの国々がエネルギー需要に対して化石燃料にいまでも大いに依存している。

Many countries still rely heavily (   ) fossil fuels for their energy needs.

4) 学生たちは勉強のための十分な時間を空けるためにアルバイトの時間を週に数時間に制限するのが望ましい。

It is advisable for students to (   ) part-time work to a few hours a week in order to free up enough time for studying.

★ TRANSLATIONS

日本語に合うように (   ) の語句を並び替えて、文を完成させなさい。

1) 高齢化につれて、長期間の介護を必要とする様々な疾患のある人がますます増えるのは避けられない。

As the population ages, it is (be / inevitable / more and more / people / that / there / will / with) various disorders needing long-term care.

_____

_____

2) 気象変動がますます多くの食料不足を引き起こすことが予測される。

It is predicted that (climate change / food / lead / to more / and more / of / shortages / will).

_____

_____

Unit 14

Droning On About Whales

クジラから放出される液体を集めて調査するために、ドローンを使い始めた科学者たちがいる。これはクジラの健康状態を把握するのに役立つそうだ。

VOCABULARY

下の単語を本文中に探し、(a) ～ (e) の中から語義としてふさわしいものをそれぞれ選びなさい。

1) whale　　**2) unmanned**　　**3) fluid**

4) visible　　**5) driver**

(a) can be seen

(b) a liquid (or sometimes a gas)

(c) operated automatically with no person present

(d) a very large animal that lives in the sea

(e) a cause of or a major influence on something

🔊 1st Listening　　まず VOA ニュースを聴きましょう。

SUMMARY CHECK

ニュースの概要として最もふさわしいものを下の 1) ～ 4) のなかから選びなさい。

1) Drone collection of whale spray is good, but it is not as effective as methods that involve killing whales.

2) Scientists have begun using drones to collect whale blow, in an effort to better understand whale health.

3) There has been an international ban on whaling since 1986.

4) Vanessa Pirotta believes that scientific progress will make it much easier to study whale health.

📝 **Notes**

Historically, sailors (¹   ) out the words "Thar she blows!" whenever they saw whales.

Today, the old cry of sailors is taking on new meaning as scientists (²   ) to modern technology to study
5 whales.

Some scientists have (³   ) using drone aircraft, also known as unmanned aerial vehicles, to collect some of the fluids expelled by whales.

Vanessa Pirotta is a researcher with Macquarie
10 University in Sydney, Australia. She told the Reuters news agency that a drone has (⁴   ) used for the first time to collect whale mucus from humpback whales at sea. She believes that drones could (⁵   ) improve scientists' understanding of whales around the world.

15 "We're collecting ... that visible plume of spray rising from the whale's blowhole, as they come to the surface to
(⁶   )," she said.

The method, she (⁷   ), could provide a better understanding of the (⁸   ) and drivers of disease in
20 wild populations.

Pirotta was one of the writers of a paper on the
(⁹   ) of drones to study whales. The paper appeared in the online publication, *Viruses*.

She and other scientists reported that they (¹⁰   )
25 whale blow from 19 humpbacks during 2017. At the time, the whales were (¹¹   ) northward from Antarctica to northern Australia.

The report said the spray is collected in a small container (¹²   ) to the top of a drone. The person
30 operating the drone opens the container just as the aircraft
(¹³   ) above the whale.

Notes column:

Thar she blows! (=There she blows!): クジラが潮を吹いたぞ。

take on new meaning: 新たな意味を帯びる

aerial vehicle: 航空機

expel: 〜を吐き出す

news agency: 通信社

mucus: 粘液
humpback whale: ザトウクジラ

plume: 水柱
spray: しぶき
blowhole: (クジラ・イルカの) 噴気孔

Viruses: 『ヴァイルシーズ』誌

Pirotta (^{14}) the new method as less invasive than using a boat to get close enough to collect fluids. And it is better than methods that depend on killing whales or
35 on whales that are (^{15}). The whale spray collected by a drone contains DNA, the (^{16}) of genetic information, proteins and different kinds of bacteria.

Pirotta said her team can collect bacteria that live in a whale's (^{17}) to measure whale health.

40 In this way, drones (^{18}) as an early-warning system of possible changes in whales' health.

An international ban on whaling took (^{19}) in 1986. But Japan announced last year that it would restart commercial whaling this July in its waters and
45 (^{20}) economic area.

invasive: 侵入する

genetic information: 遺伝情報

early-warning system: 早期警報システム

commercial whaling: 商業捕鯨
this July: 2019年7月

★ TRUE OR FALSE?

1)〜5) のなかからニュースの内容として正しいものには T、間違っているものには F を選びなさい。

1) Vanessa Pirotta is a researcher.
2) Pirotta and her team are using drones to collect whale mucus.
3) Pirotta and her team haven't yet written about their research.
4) Using drones to collect whale mucus helps scientists to understand diseases in whale.
5) Using a boat would be less invasive than using drones.

日本語に合うように (   ) を埋めなさい。

1) 商業捕鯨の国際的な禁止は 1986 年に施行されている。

An international (   ) on commercial whaling has been in place since 1986.

2) 無人航空機はドローンとして一般に知られている。

Unmanned aerial vehicles are commonly (   ) as drones.

3) 冬の数カ月間には、アラスカ周辺に生息するザトウクジラは南の赤道に向かって回遊する。

In the winter months, many humpback whales living around Alaska migrate (   ) towards the Equator.

4) データを集めるためにドローンを使用することは将来もっと浸透する可能性がある。

The use (   ) drones to collect data is likely to become more widespread in the future.

★ TRANSLATIONS

日本語に合うように (   ) の語句を並び替えて、文を完成させなさい。

1) 心臓病の主な原因は質の悪い食生活であることが一般に認識されている。

It is commonly (a major / driver / heart disease / is / of / poor diet / recognized / that).

_____

_____

2) クジラの仲間の中には、国際自然保護連合によって絶滅危惧と分類されているものもいる。

Some species (are / as / by / classified / of / threatened / whale) the International Union for Conservation of Nature.

_____

_____

Unit 15

See-Through Organs

ドイツの科学者たちが新たな技術を用いて透明な臓器をつくった。数年後には動物が生体プリントされた臓器で生きるかどうか調べるという。

VOCABULARY

下の単語を本文中に探し、(a) ～ (e) の中から語義としてふさわしいものをそれぞれ選びなさい。

1) technology　　2) transparent　　3) microscope

4) major　　5) predict

(a) a device that helps us to see very small things
(b) to guess what will happen in the future
(c) can be seen through
(d) important or large
(e) practical uses of scientific knowledge

◄)) 1st Listening　　まず VOA ニュースを聴きましょう。

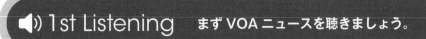

SUMMARY CHECK

ニュースの概要として最もふさわしいものを下の 1) ～ 4) のなかから選びなさい。

1) Ludwig Maximilians University in Munich is a leader in medical technologies.
2) 3D printers are becoming more and more advanced.
3) Computed tomography and magnetic resonance imaging are the best technologies for understanding internal organs.
4) Some scientists in Germany have developed transparent human organs using advanced technology.

📝 **Notes**

　Scientists in Germany say they have (¹　　　　) new technology to create see-through human organs. They say the technology could lead to production of three-dimensional body parts for (²　　　) in transplant operations.

see-through: 透けて見える
organ: 器官
three-dimensional (3D): 3次元の

operation: 手術

　The scientists are with Ludwig Maximilians University in Munich. They said they developed a (³　　　) that uses a solvent to make transparent organs, such as the (⁴　　　) and kidneys.

solvent: 溶液
transparent: 透明な
kidney: 腎臓

　The German researchers use lasers in a microscope to scan the organ to be (⁵　　　). The laser light helps them see the blood vessels and every single cell inside.

laser: レーザー

scan: ～をスキャンする、検査する
blood vessel: 血管

　The researchers use this information to print out the structure of the (⁶　　　) organ. For this, they need special (⁷　　　). They use a 3D printer to manufacture the structure — one that has height, width and (⁸　　　).

　The researchers then (⁹　　　) the printer with stem cells, which can become any kind of cell in the body. The stem cells act as "(¹⁰　　　)" in the printer. They are (¹¹　　　) into the correct position, making the organ fully operational.

stem cell: 幹細胞

operational: 操作可能な

　The (¹²　　　) of the study, Ali Erturk, described the new technology as a (¹³　　　) development for 3D printing in the medical field.

　Until now 3D-printed organs (¹⁴　　　) detailed cellular structures because they were (¹⁵　　　) on two kinds of medical scanning technology, he explained. The two are computed tomography scans and magnetic resonance imaging.

　"We can see (¹⁶　　　) every single cell is... we can

cellular: 細胞の

computed tomography (CT): コンプータ断層撮影
magnetic resonance imaging (MRI): 磁気共鳴映像法

actually replicate it (^{17}) the same," Erturk said. "I believe we are much (^{18}) to a real human organ for the first time now," he added.

35   Erturk and his team (^{19}) to start by creating a transparent, bioprinted pancreas over the next two to three years. They hope to develop a human kidney within five to six years.

    The researchers will first (^{20}) to see if animals
40 can live with bioprinted organs and could start tests within five to 10 years, he predicted.

replicate: 〜を複製する

pancreas: 膵臓

★ TRUE OR FALSE?

1) 〜 5) のなかからニュースの内容として正しいものには T、間違っているものには F を選びなさい。

1) The scientists mentioned use lasers to scan organs.
2) 3D printing is not suitable for creating the artificial organs, so the scientists use an alternative technology.
3) The purpose of the transparent organs is to help medical students understand the structure of the human body.
4) Ali Erturk is the leader of the study.
5) A pancreas and a heart are the organs the scientists plan to create in the next few years.

日本語に合うように（　　　）を埋めなさい。

1) 次の1年あるいは2年だけでなく次の10年の自分の将来について考えてみるのは良いことである。

It's good to think about your future (　　　　　　　) not only the next year or two but also the next decade.

2) 石炭の使用は次の30年以内に多くの国で一掃されると考えられている。

It is thought that coal use will be eliminated in many countries (　　　　　　) the next thirty years.

3) その会社は携帯電話やその他の持ち運び可能な装置に使用する電力効率の良いチップを製造している。

That company makes power-efficient chips for (　　　　　　) in mobile phones and other portable devices.

4) コンピュータのファイア・ウォールはウイルスやその他のマルウェア（悪意のあるソフトウェア）に対する障壁として機能する。

A computer firewall (　　　　　　) as a barrier against viruses and other malware.

日本語に合うように（　　　）の語句を並び替えて、文を完成させなさい。

1) 未来を確実に予言することは不可能だが、さまざまな状況に備えて計画を立てるのは重要である。

It (certainty / impossible / is / predict / the future / to / with), but it is important to plan for various scenarios.

_____

_____

2) ビタミンの発見は私たちの栄養の理解に対する大きな貢献だった。

The discovery of vitamins was a (contribution / major / nutrition / of / our / to / understanding).

_____

_____

All the scripts © Voice of America

Health & Environment Reports from VOA
Volume 4
VOA 健康と環境レポート 4

2020 年 4 月 10 日　　第 1 刷発行
2023 年 3 月 10 日　　第 3 刷発行

著　者　安浪誠祐／ Richard S. Lavin

発行者　森　信久
発行所　**株式会社　松 柏 社**
〒 102-0072　東京都千代田区飯田橋 1-6-1
TEL 03 (3230) 4813（代表）
FAX 03 (3230) 4857
http://www.shohakusha.com
e-mail: info@shohakusha.com

装　　帧　　小島トシノブ（NONdesign）
レイアウト　　株式会社クリエーターズ・ユニオン（一柳 茂）
組版・印刷・製本　シナノ書籍印刷株式会社

略号＝ 754
ISBN978-4-88198-754-4